Celebration
Cook Book

Nicola Tuxworth

OXFORD
UNIVERSITY PRESS

Great Clarendon Street, Oxford OX2 6DP

Oxford University Press is a department of the University of Oxford.
It furthers the University's objective of excellence in research, scholarship,
and education by publishing worldwide in

Oxford New York

Athens Auckland Bangkok Bogotá Buenos Aires Calcutta
Cape Town Chennai Dar es Salaam Delhi Florence Hong Kong Istanbul
Karachi Kuala Lumpur Madrid Melbourne Mexico City Mumbai
Nairobi Paris São Paulo Singapore Taipei Tokyo Toronto Warsaw

with associated companies in Berlin Ibadan

Oxford is a registered trade mark of Oxford University Press
in the UK and in certain other countries

Published in the United Kingdom
by Oxford University Press

Text © Nicola Tuxworth 2000

British Library Cataloguing in Publication Data

Data available

ISBN 0 19 915698 0

Available in packs
Celebrations   Pack of Six (one of each book)   ISBN 0 19 915703 0
Celebrations   Class Pack (six of each book)   ISBN 0 19 915704 9

Printed in Hong Kong

Acknowledgements

All photographs are by Mark Mason.

With thanks to St Mary and John Church of England First School, Oxford.

Illustrations by Jane Bottomley.

Contents

Pancakes..................................4

Decorated eggs 6

Pineapple ice-cream.................8

Hamburgers.........................10

Tropical fruit party punch 12

Date halva 14

Glossary 16

Index...................................16

This symbol means you will need an adult to help you.

Pancakes

People eat pancakes on Shrove Tuesday, the day before the start of Lent.

You will need

300 ml milk

a pinch of salt

brown sugar

125 g plain flour

1 large egg

sunflower oil

1 lemon

1 Put the flour, egg, salt, and half of the milk into a large bowl. ▶

2 Beat the mixture with a wooden spoon, until it is smooth. Add the rest of the milk and beat again.

3 Heat some oil. Add some pancake mixture. Tilt the pan so that the mixture covers the bottom.

4 Toss the pancake or turn it over in the pan.

5 When the pancake is cooked, put it somewhere warm. Keep cooking pancakes until the mixture is used up. Eat with lemon and sugar.

Decorated eggs

In Christian countries all over the world, eggs are cooked, decorated, and given as gifts at Easter time.

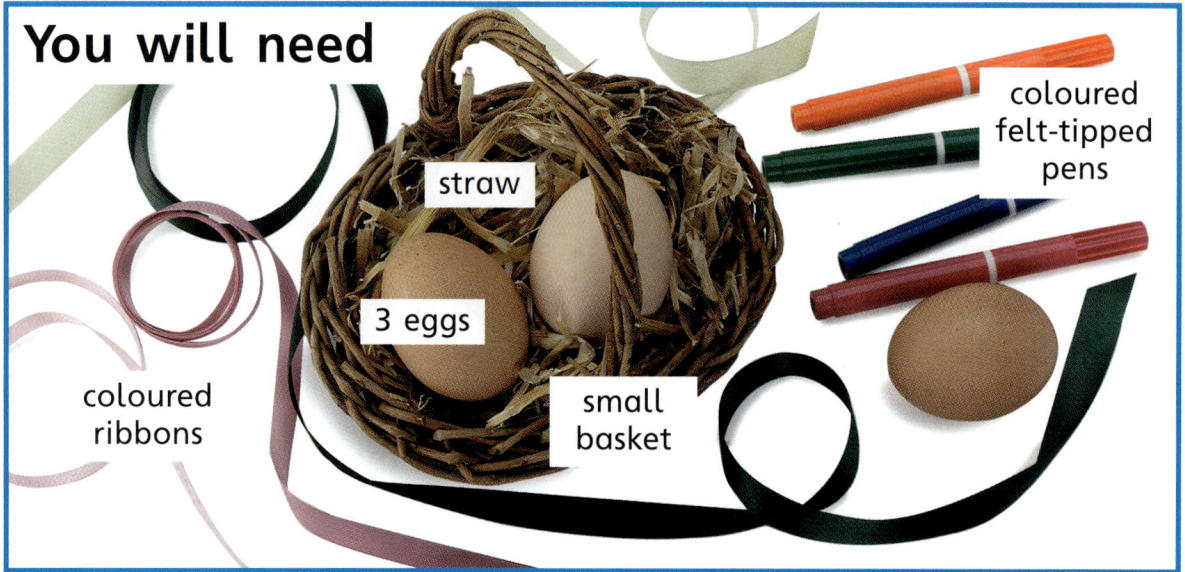

You will need

straw

3 eggs

coloured ribbons

small basket

coloured felt-tipped pens

1 Gently put the eggs into a small pan of cold water.

2 **Boil** the water and cook the eggs for 10 minutes.

3 When they are cool, decorate the eggs with pens. Draw pictures or patterns.

4 Decorate the basket with coloured ribbons. Tie a bow at each side of the handle.

5 Put some straw in the basket, and arrange the eggs carefully on the top.

Pineapple ice-cream

This sweet ice-cream is delicious. It might be eaten as part of a special meal in the Caribbean islands. It is very easy to make.

You will need

450 ml milk

175 g caster sugar

400 ml whipped cream

mint leaves for decoration

3 eggs

small can of crushed pineapple

1 Mix the eggs, milk and sugar together with a whisk.

8

2 Heat the mixture gently and stir it. When the mixture gets thicker, beat it with a whisk and leave it to cool.

3 Pour the whipped cream into the mixture, stirring it gently.

5 Pour the mixture into a plastic box, and **freeze** it for at least four hours. Decorate it with mint leaves.

4 Add the crushed pineapple and stir gently.

9

Hamburgers

Hamburgers were invented in America, and are served at parties and barbecues all year round.

You will need

crisp lettuce

soft buns

1 teaspoon each of salt and pepper

600 g of lean minced beef

sliced tomatoes

dill pickles

tomato ketchup

1 Put the meat, salt and pepper in a large bowl. **Knead** the mixture with your fingers, and make 6 round hamburgers. Wash your hands.

2 Turn the grill up to high and cook the burgers for five minutes each side, or until they are completely cooked. ▶

◀ **3** Cut each bun in half. Spread ketchup on the bottom halves.

4 Put a hamburger on the bottom half of each bun, and put the salad and pickles in layers on the burger. ▼

5 Eat while hot! ▼

Tropical fruit party punch

In hot countries, party drinks like this punch are made from **tropical** fruits and lemonade. You can use any tropical fruits to make it, so choose the ones you like best.

You will need

ice cubes

1 pineapple

1 ripe mango

1 bottle lemonade

1 lime

3 tablespoons caster sugar

1 lemon

3 kiwi fruit

1 Put the lemonade in the fridge and **freeze** two trays of ice cubes.

2 A few hours later, **peel** and slice the lemon, lime, and kiwi fruit.

3 Peel the mango and cut it into chunks. Cut the pineapple into four wedges, then peel and slice them.

4 Put the fruit into a big bowl and sprinkle with the sugar. Leave for 30 minutes.

5 Add the lemonade and the ice.

6 Stir and serve the punch.

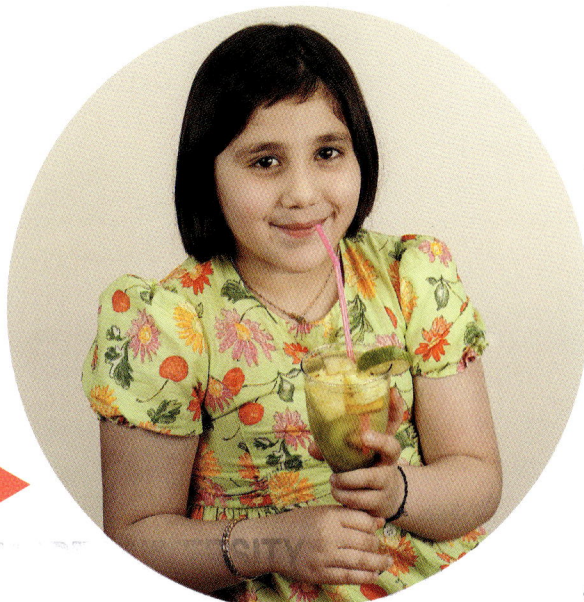

Date halva

This **sweetmeat** is from the Middle East, where it is often served with coffee at the end of a meal.

You will need

icing sugar

50 g chopped walnuts

50 g chopped almonds

250 g dates

1 Take the stones out of the dates.

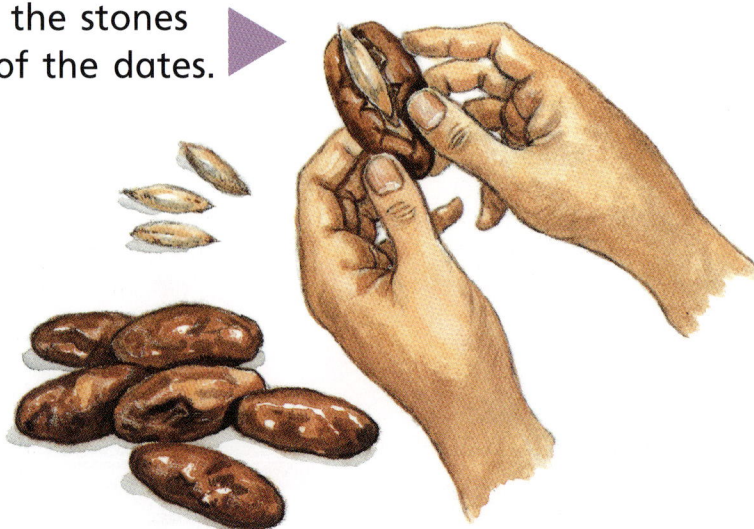

2 Chop the dates into small pieces. ▶

◀ **3** Mix the nuts and dates together in a bowl.

4 Sprinkle some icing sugar onto a board, and roll the date mixture into a sausage shape. Cut the sausage into slices. ▶

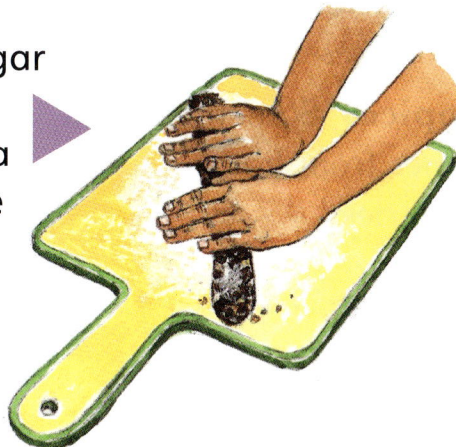

◀ **5** Arrange the slices on a plate and sprinkle some more icing sugar over the top.

Glossary

boil To heat liquid until it bubbles. Water boils at 100°C.

freeze To chill something until it becomes hard.

Index

America   10
barbecue   10
Caribbean   8
dates   14, 15
Easter   6
eggs   4, 6, 7, 8
fruit   12, 13
gifts   6
halva   14, 15
hamburgers   10, 11
ice-cream   8, 9
Lent   4
Middle East   14
pancakes   4, 5